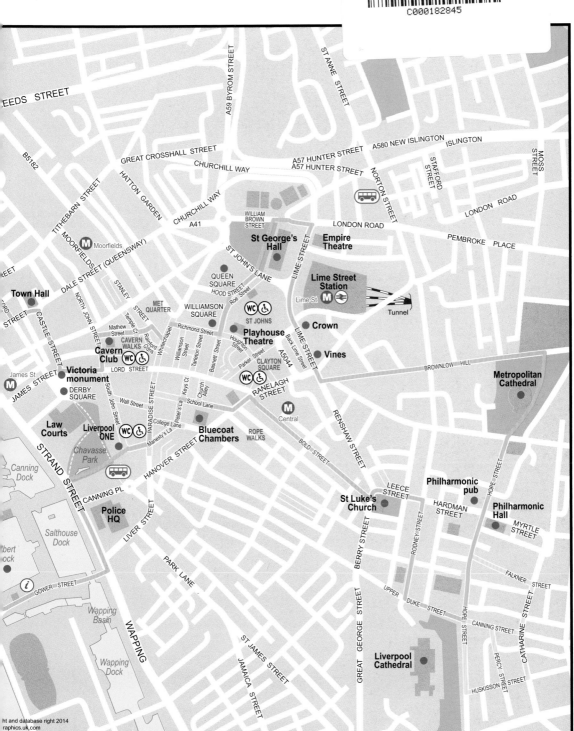

LEEDS STREET

B5182

GREAT CROSSHALL STREET

CHURCHILL WAY

A57 HUNTER STREET
A57 HUNTER STREET

A580 NEW ISLINGTON   ISLINGTON

MOSS STREET

STAFFORD STREET

NORTON STREET

A59 BYROM STREET

ST ANNE STREET

CHURCHILL WAY

A41

WILLIAM BROWN STREET

LONDON ROAD

LONDON ROAD

PEMBROKE PLACE

HATTON GARDEN

TITHEBARN STREET

M Moorfields

MOORFIELDS (QUEENSWAY)

DALE STREET

ST JOHN'S LANE

St George's Hall

Empire Theatre

LIME STREET

Lime Street Station
M

Lime St

Tunnel

Town Hall

NORTH JOHN STREET

STANLEY STREET

CASTLE STREET

NORTH STREET

QUEEN SQUARE

HOOD STREET

ROE STREET

MET QUARTER

WILLIAMSON SQUARE

Temple Ct

Mathew Street

CAVERN WALKS

Richmond Street

WHITECHAPEL

WILLIAMSON STREET

TARLETON STREET

BASNETT STREET

WC

ST JOHNS

Playhouse Theatre

HOUGHTON STREET

Crown

Vines

BACK LIME STREET

LIME STREET

A5044

BROWNLOW HILL

Cavern Club
WC

Victoria monument

M James St

JAMES STREET

DERBY SQUARE

LORD STREET

Radford Gdns

PARKER STREET

CLAYTON SQUARE

WC

Metropolitan Cathedral

Law Courts

Liverpool ONE
WC

PARADISE STREET

College Lane

St Peter's La

Keys Ct

Church Alley

School Lane

Manesty's La

Wall Street

South John Street

RANELAGH STREET

M Central

Bluecoat Chambers

ROPE WALKS

RENSHAW STREET

HOPE STREET

STRAND STREET

Chavasse Park

HANOVER STREET

BOLD STREET

Philharmonic pub

Canning Dock

Salthouse Dock

bert ock

i

GOWER STREET

Police HQ

LIVER STREET

CANNING PL

St Luke's Church

LEECE STREET

HARDMAN STREET

BERRY STREET

RODNEY STREET

Philharmonic Hall

MYRTLE STREET

FALKNER STREET

CATHARINE STREET

PERCY STREET

Wapping Basin

Wapping Dock

WAPPING

PARK LANE

ST JAMES STREET

JAMAICA STREET

GREAT GEORGE STREET

UPPER DUKE STREET

HOPE STREET

CANNING STREET

Liverpool Cathedral

HUSKISSON STREET

ht and database right 2014
raphics.uk.com

Welcome to Liverpool

Liverpool is a thriving and dynamic city. In recent times, it has been triumphantly reinventing itself as a sparkling visitor venue, with a wealth of inspirational projects that more than justify the city's traditional chirpy self-confidence. The architectural legacy of Liverpool is undoubtedly magnificent, much of it rejuvenated and restored to full glory. The city offers an eclectic mix of attractions, with fascinating, world-class museums and galleries to suit all tastes. This guide will help you share in the rich cultural heritage and experience the excitement and vibrancy that Liverpool has to offer, by exploring all that is best, old and new.

A short history

Liverpool's history is inextricably bound up with the River Mersey and the world-famous port which grew on its banks. The original 'pool' was a mile-long inlet on which King John built a castle and a church in 1207, creating a new Royal Borough. But for centuries, few merchant ships called. Nearby Chester, on the River Dee, was busier. The tide metaphorically turned when Liverpool backed the victorious Parliamentarians in the Civil War (1642–48). Royalist Chester lost out. In any case, the Dee was silting up. Other factors were at work, too: industry, founded on local coal, salt and glass, was growing and ports on the south coast were being menaced by the French.

By the mid-18th century, wealthy local families were pouring money into shipping, commerce and port-based industries. Enclosed docks were everywhere on the waterfront, and elegant streets and grand buildings were created. The inhuman slave trade brought huge wealth to the city: goods manufactured in Britain were shipped from Liverpool to West Africa and exchanged for slaves; the slaves were transported to the Americas and the ships returned to Liverpool with goods such as tobacco, cotton and sugar. Slavery was abolished in Britain in 1807, but the cotton trade boomed. Liners took millions of emigrants to new lives in North America, Australia and New Zealand. To match its prosperity as the British Empire's second port, Liverpool's Georgian heart gave way to Victorian splendour, unsanitary suburbs were cleaned up and wonderful new parks created.

But the 20th century brought economic decline. Grievously hit by competition and two world wars, Liverpool lost its status as a port, only to regain it as a vibrant city of culture. In the 1960s came the Beatles and the world-famous Merseybeat or Mersey Sound, still echoing strongly today. Then, other aspects of the arts came to the fore, with the creation of superb new galleries and museums. Following Liverpool's designation as European City of Culture, new architecture has sprung up all over the city, bringing many previously rundown areas to fresh, exciting life.

Albert Dock

Hundreds once toiled at Albert Dock, loading and unloading cargoes in and out of its splendid warehouses. Now, transformed in identity, the dock is once more at the heart of Liverpool life. It offers a unique mix of cafés, restaurants and shops, as well as fascinating museums, the unique Beatles Story (see pages 12–13), and the internationally important Tate Liverpool art gallery.

The dock and warehouses

Designed by Jesse Hartley and opened by Prince Albert in 1846, the warehouses here stored valuable cargoes in light, well-ventilated conditions. But the dock was designed for sailing ships, which were soon superseded by larger steamships needing wider access and an open quayside. By 1920, the dock was no longer used for commercial shipping and the warehouses finally closed in 1972. Plans were afoot to clear the site, but the opening of the Merseyside Maritime Museum in 1980 led the way to wholesale redevelopment. Boats from the extended Leeds and Liverpool Canal bring further new life to the water here.

Albert Dock

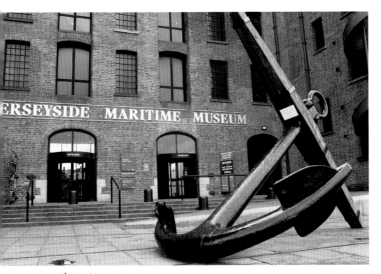

Merseyside Maritime Museum

International Slavery Museum

The International Slavery Museum was opened in 2007 to mark the 200th anniversary of the abolition of the trade in Britain. It is the world's first permanent museum dedicated to the transatlantic slave trade, demonstrating Liverpool's commitment to increasing understanding of the slave trade and its consequences.

Merseyside Maritime Museum

No visit to Liverpool is complete without exploring this superb museum. Galleries on six floors tell the story of the city's seafaring history and of life in the merchant navy. Amongst many absorbing displays, highlights include the story of the Battle of the Atlantic in the Second World War (conducted from a bunker very nearby; see page 9) and the gallery devoted to the ill-fated *Titanic*, *Lusitania* and *Empress of Ireland*.

'Breaking Free' sculpture,
International Slavery Museum

Leeds and Liverpool Canal

In 1770 an Act was passed authorizing the construction of this important waterway, although it was not until 1816 that the main line of the canal was completed. Its primary cargo was coal, and trade continued on the canal until the 1980s. In 2009 the £20 million Liverpool Canal Link was completed, reconnecting the Leeds and Liverpool Canal to Liverpool's South Docks via Stanley Dock, allowing boats to sail past Pier Head and into Albert Dock.

Tate Liverpool

Tate Liverpool

The whitened walls, wooden floors and cast-iron columns of a former Albert Dock warehouse make an ideal setting for this acclaimed collection of modern and contemporary art. Around 12,000 square metres (14,000 square yards) of galleries display a huge range of works from the Tate Collection and also from special exhibitions: painting and sculpture, of course, but also photography, prints, video, performance art and installation art.

Pier Head

Pier Head

For centuries the Pier Head was Liverpool's foremost departure point for passenger shipping. In the 19th and early 20th centuries, hundreds of thousands boarded liners here, bidding an emotional farewell to Europe in search of a better life in the New World. Now the biggest passenger ships call here once more, for Liverpool's Pier Head, with its majestic Three Graces, is one of the world's great landmarks.

The Three Graces

These are the three 20th-century buildings which give the Pier Head its identity. The first to be built was the head office of the Mersey Docks and Harbour Board, now known as the Port of Liverpool Building (1907), Italianate in style, with a Classical dome, all in Portland stone. If any one building represents Liverpool, it is the Royal Liver Building (1911), with its two copper liver birds on top. It was Britain's first multi-storey concrete-framed building. The Cunard Building in the middle (1916), built for the Cunard steamship company, shows Italian, Greek and American architectural influences.

Mann Island

Mann Island forms part of Liverpool's waterfront between the Pier Head and Albert Dock. Construction of the buildings here commenced in 2008, replacing old dockside warehouses. In sympathy with the skyline, the structures are designed to be of a similar height to the Three Graces. As well as being home to the magnificent Museum of Liverpool, you can also visit the Open Eye Gallery, an independent not-for-profit photography gallery that has a permanent archive of photographs from the 1930s onward, as well as changing exhibitions that support new and established photographers.

Museum of Liverpool

Opened in 2011, this Museum – in its landmark building on Liverpool's waterfront at the Pier Head – has won several awards, including the Council of Europe Museum Prize for 2013. Here visitors can explore how the history and culture of Liverpool's port, its people and sporting heritage have shaped the city. Set over three floors, as well as permanent galleries, there are changing exhibitions and displays, so there is always something new to see and much for all ages to enjoy.

Delve into the archaeological secrets of the city, from the Ice Age to the present day, with the interactive 'Merseyside Map' and the huge and fascinating History Detectives timeline. Amongst many other exciting exhibits, The People's Republic gallery reveals the stories of everyday people, what it means to be Liverpudlian, how people have left their mark on the city, and the impact of dramatic social change over the last 200 years. And don't miss the Wondrous Place gallery, celebrating the city's great sporting personalities and musicians – you can even have a go in the karaoke room.

Royal Liver Building, one of the Three Graces

Liverpool parish church

Sailors would come to pray at the Chapel of St Mary del Key, which stood close to the water's edge in 1257. This was replaced by the Church of Our Lady and St Nicholas (known locally as St Nick's) in the 14th century, and since then various additions have taken place including two towers (the 1746 one collapsed in 1810, killing 25 people). In December 1940 the main body of the church was destroyed by enemy air raids, but was faithfully rebuilt between 1949 and 1952.

The view from the water

Immortalized by the Gerry and the Pacemakers' song of the 1960s, the ferry across the Mersey is by far the most memorable and effective way to see Liverpool's world-famous waterfront. For only a few pounds, you can make the triangular journey from the Pier Head to two points on the Birkenhead side – a delightful breath of fresh estuary air.

Seven streets

The medieval borough of Liverpool consisted of seven streets around the castle, which stood where the Victoria monument is now. These included Castle Street, Water Street and Chapel Street, at the heart of Liverpool's business district. This area includes Liverpool's splendid Georgian Town Hall, one of the oldest buildings in the city centre, as well as some very grand monuments and commercial buildings.

Town Hall

Liverpool's first town hall, built in 1515, was little more than a thatched barn, but it served the town for over 150 years. Poor foundations saw to it that a stone successor, built in 1673, was short-lived. The present Town Hall was originally designed in 1754 by John Wood, principal architect of Bath's magnificent streets. It has been substantially altered over the years, not least by James Wyatt who added the splendid dome and the Corinthian portico. It is worth going inside to look at the superb entrance hall, staircase and dome interior.

Nelson Memorial

To the rear of the Town Hall, you will find Liverpool's oldest outdoor monument (1813), funded by public donation, notably from anti-slavery campaigner William Roscoe. Besides commemorating Nelson and his four great naval achievements, the bronze monument celebrated the city's growing international prestige and also reminded Liverpool's merchants of the freedom that Nelson had won.

Town Hall

Town Hall entrance

Still almost a secret

The Western Approaches Museum is a massive underground bunker off Rumford Street. Between 1941 and 1945, 400 people from three combined services toiled here in secret to protect Allied convoys against German U-boats in the Battle of the Atlantic. Impossible to demolish economically, for nearly half a century the bunker remained as it was left when the war ended. You can now explore the underground labyrinth of rooms several days a week between March and the end of October.

India Buildings

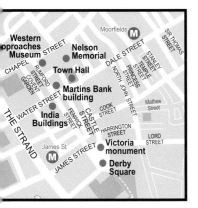

India Buildings and Martins Bank building

Of many fine commercial buildings in this area of Liverpool, two on our route, both by architect Herbert Rowse, deserve particular mention. India Buildings (1923) on Water Street, built for the Blue Funnel Line, is an American-influenced block, notable for its wonderful vaulted arcade. The former Martins Bank building (1932), also close to the Town Hall on Water Street, is undoubtedly one of the finest bank buildings in Europe, primarily art deco with American, French and Egyptian influences. Bronze doors lead to an arcaded, cathedral-like banking hall of Travertine marble where Rowse has explored the theme of maritime money down to the last detail.

Monument to Queen Victoria

Mocked for its conservatism when completed in 1906, the monument presides over Derby Square where Liverpool Castle once stood. The fine sculptures represent agriculture, commerce, education and industry below, and wisdom, justice, charity and peace above. On top of the dome is the figure of Fame.

Martins Bank building detail

9

The Cavern Quarter

After the Second World War, central Liverpool lay in ruins and shipping was in decline. It was the Beatles who put Liverpool back on the world map, and it's the Cavern Club in Mathew Street, at the heart of the vibrant Cavern Quarter, that is indelibly associated with the group. This exciting venue is the ultimate place of pilgrimage for Beatles fans who visit in their thousands from around the globe.

The Cavern Club

The Cavern Club opened in the late 1950s as a jazz club, and it was in that era that John Lennon and Paul McCartney first appeared here – playing skiffle. Gradually, beat music took over, and the Cavern became the epicentre of the booming Merseybeat scene. In all, the Beatles performed here 292 times. The club was forced to close in 1973, the warehouse above demolished and the cellar filled in. However, in 1984 the Cavern was rebuilt on the same site using the original bricks. Since then the club has reasserted itself as a leading live music venue. The owners of the Cavern run the nearby Hard Day's Night Hotel and also the Magical Mystery Tour (see page 30) which leaves from nearby Whitechapel to tour the other key Beatles locations in the suburbs (see pages 12–13).

Inside the Cavern at a lunchtime performance by the Beatles in 1961

Mathew Street

Two walls of fame

Forming the façade of the Cavern Pub is the Cavern Wall of Fame, which opened in 1997 on the 40th anniversary of the Cavern Club opposite. The wall displays the names of many artistes who have appeared at the Cavern since 1957. Nearby, the pink Liverpool wall of fame celebrates all the city's No.1 hits since 1952.

Two pubs with Beatles links

In the early 1960s the Cavern served no alcohol, so the Beatles and other groups used to repair to The Grapes and the White Star before and after performances. The Grapes displays a picture of the Beatles in the pub in 1961. The Victorian White Star is in superb original condition. One story has it that its back room was where the Beatles and other Cavern acts were paid. It has a plaque commemorating its Beatles links.

John Lennon statue by the Cavern Wall of Fame

Cavern Walks

The Mathew Street façade of this shopping development is designed as a permanent monument to the Beatles, and many of its features were the idea of John Lennon's first wife, Cynthia. Amongst other attractions in the shopping centre is the life-size statue of the Beatles by sculptor John Doubleday (born 1947) in the central atrium.

'Four lads who shook the world'

The Beatle Street statue in Mathew Street was created in 1974 by local sculptor Arthur Dooley. The Madonna was originally depicted with the Beatles as four cherubs, but fans have removed the one representing Paul. A guitar-carrying cherub with a 'Lennon lives' halo was added after John's death.

Beatles landmarks

John, Paul, George and Ringo grew up in and around Liverpool, playing together in their early years, not just at the Cavern but at many church halls and dance halls in the area. Many locations in the city and its suburbs survive as reminders of their lives and their music.

The Beatles Story

This extremely popular attraction is housed on two sites. The main part of the Beatles Story is set in the basement of one of Albert Dock's refurbished warehouses, and brings together many of the major events in the lives of the 'Fab Four'. A cleverly worked warren of scenarios, with voices, music, commentary, video clips and genuine artefacts, unfolds the story of how four ordinary Scousers became the greatest band in the world. The journey takes you from John and Paul's first meeting at a village fête in Woolton, all the way through the years of Beatlemania, to the band's break-up and their musical lives after they went their separate ways.

Just a short distance away, the Beatles Story Pier Head, in the Mersey Ferries terminal, is where visitors can enjoy special exhibitions and revel in the Fab4D Experience, where the Beatles' music is brought to life in magical 4D in a state-of-the-art theatre.

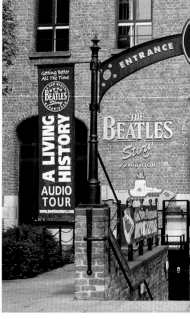

The Beatles Story, Albert Dock

Suburbs full of echoes

In Woolton, south-east of the city centre, you will find 'Mendips' (251 Menlove Avenue, Woolton), where John lived with his Aunt Mimi from 1945 to 1963. A mile away in Allerton is 20 Forthlin Road, Paul's childhood home. Both houses are now owned by the National Trust and internal tours are bookable online with them. In the same area you will find the 'shelter in the middle of a roundabout', at the end of Penny Lane, and the gates to Strawberry Field (a former orphanage on Beaconsfield Road). George Harrison lived at 12 Arnold Grove, Wavertree, while Ringo was born at 9 Madryn Street in the suburb of Dingle.

John Lennon's piano, The Beatles Story

The Casbah Coffee Club

This is one of the lesser known, but least spoiled and most significant, Beatles locations. In the basement of 8 Haymans Green in picturesque West Derby village, Mona Best, mother of the Beatles' first drummer Pete Best, opened a coffee club in 1959. The Quarrymen, the band that evolved into the Beatles, played at the opening night. The Casbah was also the venue for the Beatles' first gig after learning their trade in Germany, a sensational rebirth which shook the city and led to their 'discovery' at the Cavern. Almost all the famous Liverpool groups played at the Casbah at one time or another. Miraculously surviving just as it was in those days, with ceilings painted by various Beatles, it is now an English Heritage Grade II listed site open for pre-booked tours.

The Beatles Story

Eleanor Rigby statue, Stanley Street

20 Forthlin Road, Paul McCartney's childhood home

All the lonely people

In Stanley Street, not far from the Cavern Quarter, is a bronze figure of Eleanor Rigby of Beatles' song fame. The work of 1950s and '60s pop star Tommy Steele, it was given to the city in 1982. Inside it are said to be objects to imbue Eleanor with magical properties: a page from the Bible for spirituality, sonnets for love, a clover leaf for luck, and so on.

St George's Quarter

The new millennium, World Heritage status and the European City of Culture award brought a rekindling of interest and enthusiasm in Liverpool's great buildings. St George's Quarter has enjoyed state-of-the-art modernization and the restoration of splendour to the massive and magnificent St George's Hall.

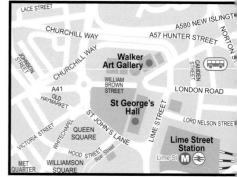

St George's Hall

Designed by Harvey Elmes, completed by Charles Cockerell in 1854 and restored in 2007, St George's Hall is widely acclaimed as the finest neo-classical building in Europe. No one should pass its grand portico without taking a (free) look at the breathtaking Great Hall, with its gilded ceilings, porphyry arcading and Minton tile floor (which is sadly not always on display). Here dazzling balls were held and Charles Dickens read extracts from his latest novels. Here too were the city's law courts, scene of many a murder trial. Visitors can retrace the steps of unfortunate prisoners from the cells to the dock … and back.

The sculpture room, Walker Art Gallery

Walker Art Gallery

Without exaggeration, the Walker Art Gallery has one of Europe's greatest collections of fine and decorative art. Here, in a warren of rooms, are displays of hundreds of works from the masters of the Renaissance to the present day. The brewer Sir Andrew Barclay Walker was better known for building grand public houses than for collecting art, but in 1873 he donated £20,000 for the building of a new gallery which was to bear his name. The building underwent a major refurbishment from 1999 to 2002.

'Sense of Sight' (1895) by Annie Louisa Swynnerton, Walker Art Gallery

Above: St George's Hall

Left: The Great Hall, St George's Hall

The Walker's beautiful sculpture room by the entrance is an unforgettable and essential experience. Elsewhere in the gallery there are many fine examples of European art and a major collection of Victorian paintings of which the Pre-Raphaelite works are outstanding. The modern collection is also stunning, with paintings by household names such as Lucian Freud and David Hockney.

St George's Plateau

St George's Plateau, the area before the elegant façade of St George's Hall, has long been a gathering place for Liverpudlians at great moments in time. Here regiments have gathered before marching off to war, strikers have protested and victorious football teams have been welcomed home.

In addition to the war memorial, three statues stand out here: Queen Victoria and her consort Prince Albert are each mounted on horseback (both statues are the work of Thomas Thornycroft), while Liverpool's Major-General William Earle strides into battle from a plinth near the south steps. Earle, from Allerton, was killed in the Sudan in 1885 while trying to rescue General Gordon from Khartoum.

Prince Albert statue, St George's Plateau

William Brown Street

The most complete manifestation of Liverpool's one-time wealth is to be found in the area around William Brown Street and the St George's Quarter, with their magnificent neo-classical buildings created to reflect the city's internationally celebrated patronage of the arts in Victorian times.

St John's Garden

The garden, opened in 1904, is a 'green lung' in the heart of the city. The original idea of a sculptor, George Frampton, it is home to one of the finest collections of outdoor monuments of the early 20th century. Notable amongst the statues are those of W.E. Gladstone, born in Liverpool, four times Prime Minister; William Rathbone, Member of Parliament and founder of the district nursing movement and the universities of Liverpool and Wales; and the memorial to the King's Liverpool Regiment commemorating their service in the South African War.

St John's Garden

World Museum

Central Library

Liverpool's Central Library shares the same Grade II listed building as the World Museum. It found a temporary home while modernization was taking place, reopening in 2013 after beautiful remodelling. Here you can enjoy everything from rare books in the magnificent Hornby Library, Oak Room and Picton Reading Room to playing on an Xbox, or having coffee on the terrace overlooking St John's Garden.

Fine adornments

This area is notable for several attractive additions to its elegant landscape, including a Doric column, erected in 1863 to commemorate the Duke of Wellington, soldier and statesman. Beneath it is the cast-iron Steble Fountain of 1879, named after a mayor of the city. Interestingly, a replica of this fountain stands in front of the Massachusetts State House in Boston, USA.

Wellington's Column and the Steble Fountain

World Museum

Liverpool has the world's only 'World Museum', combining historic treasures from across the globe with the latest interactive technology, excellent for adults and children. This flagship museum has internationally important collections that give an insight into the world, both human and natural, and into our place in space and time. Amongst the highlights is the new Bug House which gives the visitor an insect's eye view of the world; it also features amazing animatronic models of creepy-crawlies. The superb aquarium allows you to see live exhibits at very close quarters.

Liverpool's overseas links have resulted in the World Cultures galleries, one of the country's top collections, reflecting the lives of people around the globe. The Planetarium, traditionally a favourite here, offers a magical half-hour trip around the universe. The Weston Discovery Centre is very much a hands-on place for adults as well as children. Members of staff are available to demonstrate, and visitors young and old have a chance to handle ancient artefacts and explore interactively the things that have fascinated them elsewhere in this splendid museum.

Metropolitan Cathedral

In 1933, on a site between Brownlow Hill and Mount Pleasant, the foundation stone was laid of the Metropolitan Cathedral of Christ the King. It was to be a truly immense Catholic cathedral, designed by Sir Edwin Lutyens. By 1958 the crypt was finished, but the cost of completing the massive scheme was prohibitive. A competition was held for a new design, and in 1960 Sir Frederic Gibberd's famous 'wigwam' concept was chosen.

The nave

The circular nave emphasizes the modernity of the cathedral. The high altar and sanctuary is accessible to the entire congregation of 2,300, with the archbishop on his presidential chair (or cathedra) at the heart of proceedings. The bronze figure of Christ is by Dame Elisabeth Frink (as is that above the west door in the Anglican Liverpool Cathedral; see pages 22–23). Through masterful use of stained glass in the lofty corona and the vertical spaces between the great concrete buttresses, the main body of the cathedral has a mystical, dark atmosphere. Royal blue light is punctuated by other rich, bright colours; beams of sunlight fall onto Italian marble floors.

Aerial view of the Metropolitan Cathedral

Edwin Lutyens' original design

The circular nave

The 'rolling stone' entrance door to the Chapel of Relics

Epic size

Lutyens' original design for the Metropolitan Cathedral was so monumental in scale that the nearby Liverpool University clock tower would have fitted within the main arch of the cathedral's entrance porch. The tower of Liverpool Cathedral rises to 101 metres (331 feet), while Lutyens' dome would have been over 50 metres (190 feet) higher.

The way of the Cross

The stations of the Cross, the stages of Christ's journey to Calvary, adorn 14 of the cathedral's giant buttresses. Cast in manganese bronze, these moving and imaginative pieces are the work of artist Sean Rice. Rice also created the ambo (or lectern) of sea eagles, the statue of Shemaiah in the crypt and the statue of Abraham in the West Apse, the head of which is said to bear a distinct resemblance to the sculptor himself.

The chapels

Each of the chapels circling the nave has its own beauty and character. Notable amongst them are the Baptistry, with bronze gates presented by the city; the Chapel of the Blessed Sacrament, containing a statue of the risen Christ by Arthur Dooley; the Chapel of Unity, dominated by the mosaic of the Pentecost by George Mayer-Marton; the Lady Chapel, with a statue of the Madonna and Child by Robert Brumby; and the Children's Chapel, with its sculpture depicting Christ with the children, created by Stephen Foster.

The crypt

No visit to the Metropolitan Cathedral is complete without asking to see the crypt, the only part of Lutyens' design to reach fruition. The Pontifical Hall in the crypt now contains archives and displays illustrating the cathedral's history. With its dark brickwork and high barrel-vaulted ceilings, it gives a flavour of the scale and grandeur of Lutyens' original design, as does the marbled Chapel of Relics containing the tombs of three archbishops.

The Hope Street Quarter

Liverpool has so many attractions and architectural delights that visitors are often unaware that on the doorstep of its two wonderful cathedrals the city possesses magnificent residential streets on a par with any that Bath or London have to offer. They are so unspoilt that film and TV companies are frequently drawn here.

Canning

Now known as Canning, Liverpool 8 was the district, created from almost open country, to which many of Liverpool's upwardly mobile merchants and professional classes moved in the early 19th century. En route between the two cathedrals, one has the chance to explore this area, including Canning Street, Gambier Terrace, Huskisson Street and Percy Street. The route back to the city centre, after visiting Liverpool Cathedral, takes you along Rodney Street, the earliest of the Georgian streets.

Decoration in the Philharmonic Hall

Rodney Street

Philharmonic Hall

The original hall, built in 1849, was destroyed by fire in 1933 but rebuilt in art deco splendour within six years. It still serves as a concert hall and cinema with a unique hydraulically operated rising screen. There is even a cinema organ which emerges in traditional style. Whether or not there is a performance, it is worth visiting the sumptuous foyer bar and the wonderful auditorium with its classic rippled ceiling.

Mr Hardman's Photographic Studio

The elegant doors and balconies of Liverpool's Hope Street Quarter hide a unique museum. For decades Edward Chambré Hardman was Liverpool's premier photographer, living and working from 59 Rodney Street. His work was portrait photography but his hobby was taking landscapes.

Two things make Hardman special today: his legacy of thousands of photographs and his studio home, by great good fortune preserved as he left it on his death in 1988. Now visitors can not only see the photographs and processes of yesteryear but also the cluttered details of Mr and Mrs Hardman's domestic life 50 and more years ago.

Everyman Theatre

The original Everyman Theatre was founded in 1964 in Hope Hall, and in the 1970s it launched the careers of actors who today are household names, including Julie Walters, Bill Nighy and Pete Postlethwaite. Following a £27 million refurbishment, the new Everyman reopened in 2014 with a production of *Twelfth Night*. The Portrait Wall on the front of the new theatre incorporates images of 150 people of all ages who represent the whole city, to emphasize the message that 'the Everyman is and always will be for everyone'.

Philharmonic pub

Philharmonic pub

Diagonally opposite the Philharmonic Hall is this superb pub, one of the most ornate in Britain. It was built at the end of the 19th century by brewery architect Walter Aubrey Thomas, styled as dining rooms to protect the sensitivities of the grandees who patronized it. Granite pillars and wrought-iron gates lead one to a wonderful art nouveau interior: stained glass, mosaic floors, copper panels, ornate mahogany panelling, moulded plaster ceilings and art nouveau tiles. There are two snugs and a very grand lounge.

A Case History

The Liverpool Institute of Performing Arts (LIPA), based in Mount Street, was the brainchild of Beatle Paul McCartney. He is just one of the 'owners' featured in *A Case History* (1998) by John King, the concrete luggage on the corner of Mount Street and Hope Street. All 27 of the cases remember people who have contributed to Liverpool's culture in some way.

Liverpool Cathedral

One of the finest and largest Anglican cathedrals in the world, Liverpool Cathedral dominates the city, not just because of its hilltop position on St James's Mount but also because of its breathtaking size. Marvellous, too, are the wonderful details within – stonework, windows, monuments, artwork. Commissioned in 1903 and completed in 1978, the cathedral became the life's work of architect Sir Giles Gilbert Scott. The 'Great Space' video and audio tour provides a superb introduction to the building.

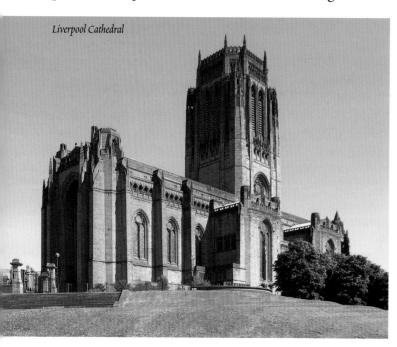

Liverpool Cathedral

The Central Space from the Nave Bridge

The tower

Scott's first plan for two smaller towers evolved into a taller, refined, single tower just over 101 metres (331 feet) high. With two lifts and 108 steps, the tower is open to the public. The 'Tower Experience' offers wonderful panoramic views over the city and river, and includes an embroidery gallery and a close-up of the magnificent bells, the highest and heaviest ringing peal in the world. The circle of marble in the main aisle represents the base outline of Great George, the largest bell, which is tolled only on special occasions.

The nave and chancel

The poet John Betjeman called Liverpool Cathedral 'one of the great buildings of the world'. Amongst many awesome views, the finest is of the soaring nave and chancel from the Nave Bridge at the west end. The east window above the altar depicts the Tree of Life, while the stained glass depicts the *Te Deum* ('We praise thee O God'). The window is so huge that the entire Lady Chapel would fit through it.

Works of art

The cathedral itself is a work of art, and within it are many smaller, but no less magnificent, pieces. Those of special note include Dame Elisabeth Frink's *The Welcoming Christ* above the west door; the reredos (altar piece), in which the figures in the representation of the Last Supper are life size or bigger; the paintings in the choir stalls, based on the parables; the ecclesiastical embroidery in the tower gallery; and the 15th-century statue of the Virgin Mary in the Lady Chapel, by Giovanni della Robbia.

'Te Deum' window

The Lady Chapel

The Lady Chapel at the cathedral's north-east corner was the first part to be completed (in 1910). Visitors appreciate its beauty, calm and intimacy, especially if the main body of the cathedral is busy. Almost every monument and window in the chapel is dedicated to women, among them Kitty Wilkinson and Agnes Jones who worked tirelessly for Liverpool's poor in the 19th century.

Big and small

With 10,268 pipes, the cathedral organ is one of the world's largest musical instruments. Its biggest pipe is 10 metres (32 feet) tall, its smallest just under 2 centimetres (¾ inch). Intriguingly, a traditional red telephone box, the smallest structure designed by Sir Giles Gilbert Scott, stands within the cathedral, his largest. It is on display by the tower lift.

Telephone box designed by Scott

Other landmarks

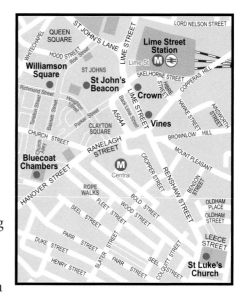

As you follow the route around the city centre you will pass Liverpool's most important tourist attractions as well as several other interesting landmarks, including the attractively renovated Williamson Square and two wonderful pubs in Lime Street. As you return to Albert Dock from Liverpool Cathedral (see pages 22–23), you will encounter a bombed-out church and central Liverpool's oldest building, now home to an exciting, expanded arts centre.

Williamson Square
In 2004, Williamson Square was transformed from little more than a taxi rank to a splendid focal point and meeting place. Pride of place goes to the arched fountains, beautifully lit at night. The square is home to the Playhouse Theatre, Merseyside's only active Victorian theatre, which is run in conjunction with the Everyman Theatre in Hope Street.

Lime Street's splendid pubs
A few of Liverpool's pubs are amongst the most palatial in Britain. The Philharmonic pub see page 21) is one, while two others stand within a short distance of each other near Lime Street Station, on the route from the St George's Quarter to the Metropolitan Cathedral. The Crown is a Victorian gin palace with a particularly fine plaster ceiling, while the Vines is even grander – an essay in Edwardian baroque splendour.

Williamson Square and St John's Beacon

Bold Street and St Luke's Church

Grand Central

Alternative shopping

To a Liverpudlian, the name Quiggins conjures up a unique and atmospheric warren of alternative shops and stalls where you can buy wacky fashions, leather, jewellery and even retro video games. Although city centre developments closed the original Quiggins, many of the traders found a new home in Grand Central, a Grade II listed building in Renshaw Street.

The bombed-out church

St Luke's Church at the top of Bold Street, gutted by an incendiary bomb in May 1941, has been left as a memorial to the Blitz in Liverpool, its churchyard a public park. A recent addition is the memorial to those who died in the Irish potato famine, which lasted from 1845 to 1852.

Bluecoat Chambers

This fine Queen Anne building in School Lane, the oldest building in the city centre, is the ancient gem of Liverpool, built between 1717 and 1725. For almost two centuries a school, it became for a while Liverpool University's architecture department. Damaged by the Blitz, it was restored to become an arts centre and meeting place. It has now been renovated and enlarged to include a new art gallery and performance space.

St John's Beacon

Visible from almost all parts of the city centre, St John's Beacon rises to 133 metres (436 feet) above the St John's Square shopping centre. It was built in the 1960s as a revolving restaurant, observation deck and ventilation shaft for the shopping centre below. These days it is home to Radio City, one of Merseyside's independent radio stations. Tours can be booked through the Tourist Information Centre (see page 30).

Bluecoat Chambers

Around the suburbs

Liverpool's centre is rich in places to visit, but the city's suburbs also have many attractions. Several of these, including the Williamson Tunnels, various Beatles locations (see pages 12–13), Sefton Park and Speke Hall, can be found south-east of the city centre.

The Palm House, Sefton Park

Sefton Park

With its lawns, lakes and woodland, Sefton Park is a lovely place to stroll, sit or play. However, pride of place must go to the Palm House (1896), a Grade I listed three-tier Victorian glasshouse now restored to its original glory. It contains a rare collection of plants from all over the world. Nearby is a celebrated statue of Peter Pan (1928) by Sir George Frampton.

An unsolved mystery

A real curiosity: brick-lined tunnels excavated in the local sandstone by hundreds of men over thirty-odd years … for no apparent reason. The instigator, eccentric timber merchant Joseph Williamson (1769–1840), seems to have commissioned the digging to give work to the many men who returned from the Napoleonic Wars to find themselves unemployed. After Williamson's death, the tunnels became repositories for unsavoury refuse and have only gradually been revealed. The Williamson Tunnels can be visited from Smithdown Lane near Liverpool University.

The Calderstones

Around 4 miles (6 kilometres) south-east of Liverpool is Calderstones Park. Here in Harthill Greenhouses in this public park you can see six highly decorated Neolithic boulders, thought to have once formed part of a chambered tomb. These extraordinary stones depict artistic symbols including spirals, concentric circles, arcs, cup and ring marks, and footprints. Originally situated just outside the park gates, the stones were moved in 1954 to protect them from further erosion.

Sudley House

Sudley House, situated just 4 miles (6 kilometres) south-east of Liverpool's city centre, was built for rich corn merchant and one-time Liverpool mayor Nicholas Robinson in the first quarter of the 19th century. This is one of the few period homes decorated in the Victorian style to retain many of its original features, and has the only surviving Victorian merchant art collection in Britain that still hangs in its original location. On the ground floor there are works by many artists, including Turner, Rossetti and Holman Hunt. On the first floor visitors can explore the childhood room, costume room and small world room along with a variety of changing exhibitions.

Two fine halls

Two historic halls hide in Liverpool's suburbs. Speke Hall, near the airport, is one of Britain's most famous Tudor manor houses: a classic black-and-white oak-framed building with rich elements of the original Tudor house, plus Jacobean plasterwork and arts and crafts influences. Croxteth Hall, the ancestral home of the Earls of Sefton until the death of the last Earl in 1972, is set in a country park near picturesque West Derby village in north-east Liverpool. Here visitors step back in time to Edwardian days.

Speke Hall

The 'Paisley Gateway', Anfield

A sporting city

As well as being home to Aintree, the venue for the world-famous steeplechase the Grand National, Liverpool has two top football teams. Both football clubs offer the chance of a 'behind-the-scenes' tour (see page 30). At Liverpool FC, in Anfield, north of the city centre, museum-only visits do not need to be pre-booked, but booking in advance is recommended for stadium tours. The same applies for the tour at Goodison Park, home of Everton FC, which is less than a mile away across Stanley Park.

Statue of legendary Everton player Dixie Dean, Goodison Park

Around the Liverpool area

Although there is much to entertain visitors in Liverpool and its suburbs, the surrounding area offers a huge variety of places to visit which reflect the region's scenic qualities, industrial heritage and creative drive.

Southport

Port Sunlight

In 1888, William Hesketh Lever built a soap factory on the Wirral and established a delightful purpose-built garden village for his employees. Today, Unilever is a household name and Port Sunlight remains a lovely place to live and visit.

Unique and attractive homes, public buildings and memorials grace lawns and open spaces: an oasis of peace within a busy area. The Port Sunlight Museum tells Port Sunlight's story. Nationally famous, the Lady Lever Art Gallery in the village is an elegant treasure house of paintings, furniture and ceramics. Its Wedgwood Jasperware collection is the finest in the world.

Lady Lever Art Gallery, Port Sunlight

Red squirrel, Freshfield Nature Reserve

Formby Point

At Formby Point, the nature reserve at Freshfield is one of the most popular attractions in the North. Here amongst the pine trees, the red squirrels are so used to visitors that they will often come very close indeed.

Southport

Just up the coast from Liverpool, Southport is an upmarket seaside resort famed for its shopping (elegant Lord Street), its seafront (now restored), its superb seaside golf courses (Royal Birkdale, Ainsdale and others) and its Victorian pleasure pier (Britain's second longest). The town hosts many annual festivals and events.

World of Glass, St Helens

Crosby

At the northern end of Liverpool is Crosby, once little known beyond Merseyside but now a place of national significance, thanks to sculptor Antony Gormley's installation 'Another Place'. One hundred lonely life-sized figures cast in iron stare out across the sands of Liverpool Bay, a haunting and very special sight which changes with every tide and season.

St Helens

St Helens is synonymous with glass-making, an industry in this town since the 18th century. The World of Glass is a stunning, award-winning visitor attraction which uses state-of-the-art special effects and live glass-blowing demonstrations to bring glass, its history, its uses and its creative potential to life. Beautiful exhibits of the internationally renowned Pilkington Glass collection and the St Helens Heritage collection tell the story of what made the town the world centre of glass.

Chester

Historic Chester, less than an hour from Liverpool by rail or road, is worthy of several days' visit in its own right. The Rows, black-and-white 'double-decker' shopping streets, are unique to the city, drawing visitors from all over the world. Other attractions include the finest city walls in Britain, the cathedral and the lovely River Dee.

Antony Gormley's 'Another Place', Crosby

The place the sea forgot

A Victorian seaside resort, Parkgate on the Wirral now looks across to North Wales over a grassy landscape. These days only at the highest tide does the water make it to the sea wall. Despite this, the place still retains its 'away-from-it-all' feel and is popular with locals who come to sit, take the air and sample the locally made ice cream.

Information

i **Tourist Information Centres**
Anchor Courtyard, Albert Dock, Liverpool L3 4BS and
Information Desk, Liverpool John Lennon Airport,
Speke Hall Road, Speke, Liverpool L24 1YD
tel: 0151 233 2008 website: www.visitliverpool.com

Shopmobility
For the use of powered wheelchairs and scooters for
those with limited mobility. Based in Liverpool ONE
(0151 707 0877) and St John's Shopping Centre
(0151 707 0877).

Liverpool attractions
The Beatles Story: 0151 709 1963, www.beatlesstory.com;
Casbah Coffee Club: 0151 280 3519,
www.casbahcoffeeclub.com;
The Cavern Club: www.cavernclub.org;
Croxteth Hall: 0151 233 3020,
http://liverpoolcityhalls.co.uk/croxteth-hall;
Everyman Theatre: 0151 709 4776 (box office),
www.everymanplayhouse.com;
International Slavery Museum: 0151 478 4499,
www.liverpoolmuseums.org.uk/ism;
Lady Lever Art Gallery: 0151 478 4136,
www.liverpoolmuseums.org.uk/ladylever;
Liverpool Cathedral: 0151 709 6271,
www.liverpoolcathedral.org.uk;
Liverpool ONE: 0151 232 3100,
www.liverpool-one.com;
Merseyside Maritime Museum: 0151 478 4999,
www.liverpoolmuseums.org.uk/maritime;
Metropolitan Cathedral: 0151 709 9222,
www.liverpoolmetrocathedral.org.uk;
Mr Hardman's Photographic Studio:
0151 709 6261, www.nationaltrust.org.uk;
Museum of Liverpool: 0151 478 4545,
www.liverpoolmuseums.org.uk/mol;
Open Eye Gallery: 0151 236 6768,
www.openeye.org.uk;
Port Sunlight Museum and Garden Village:
0151 644 6466, www.portsunlightvillage.com;
Speke Hall: 0151 427 7231, www.nationaltrust.org.uk;
Sudley House: 0151 478 4016,
www.liverpoolmuseums.org.uk/sudley;
Tate Liverpool: 0151 702 7400,
www.tate.org.uk/visit/tate-liverpool;

Walker Art Gallery: 0151 478 4199,
www.liverpoolmuseums.org.uk/walker;
Western Approaches Museum:
0151 227 2008,
www.liverpoolwarmuseum.co.uk;
Williamson Tunnels: 0151 709 6868,
www.williamsontunnels.co.uk;
World Museum Liverpool:
0151 478 4393,
www.liverpoolmuseums.org.uk/wml;
World of Glass: 01744 22766,
www.worldofglass.com.

Tours and trips
Below is a small selection of the tours
and trips available. Information on
these and many others, including walking
and cycling tours, can be obtained from
the Tourist Information Centres or
www.visitliverpool.com.

Cavern City Tours: 0151 236 9091,
www.cavernclub.org/cavern-citytours;
Cavern Magical Mystery Tour:
0151 703 9100, www.cavernclub.org/
the-magical-mystery-tour;
City Sightseeing open-top bus tour:
01789 299123, www.city-sightseeing.com;
Everton FC Stadium Tour Experience:
0151 530 5212,
www.evertonfc.com/tickets;
Liverpool FC Tour and Museum:
0151 260 6677, www.liverpoolfc.com/
history/tour-and-museum;
**Liverpool Hop-On-Hop-Off open-top
bus tour:** 0203 355 1240,
www.hop-on-hop-off-bus.com;
Mersey Ferries: 0151 330 1444,
www.merseyferries.co.uk;
**Radio City Tower Viewing Gallery
Experience:** 0151 233 2008, www.visitliv-
erpool.com/things-to-do/attractions;
Queensway Tunnel Tours:
0151 330 4504, www.merseytravel.gov.uk/
promotions-attractions.

Index of attractions

The Grand National

The world's most famous steeplechase is held at Aintree in April each year, the culmination of a three-day meeting. One highlight for visitors is the chance to view the jumps close up by walking the course on the morning of the big race.

Queensway Tunnel

Liverpool is famed for its early rail and road tunnel links. You can learn about the construction of one Mersey road tunnel, opened by King George V and Queen Mary in 1934, on a Queensway Tunnel Tour. Go behind the scenes to visit the control room and walk under the road surface – and discover why these unique tunnels have featured in Hollywood films.

Front cover: Mann Island, Liverpool.
Back cover: Royal Liver Building

Acknowledgements

Photography by kind permission of: Alamy: 5b (Vic Pigula), 11tr, 20r (Paul Thompson Images), 11bl (Bill Bachmann), 18r, 24, 25tl (Andy Marshall), 21tl (David Lyons), 21br (Eryrie), 26 (Richard Watson), 28br (Warwick Sloss), 29b (Tony Wright/earthscapes); Bridgeman Art Library: 16b (Walker Art Gallery, Liverpool); Cavern Club/Cavern City Tours: 10bl; Ron Davies: 6–7, 8, 10–11, 16bl, 17br, 17tr, 25tr; iStock: FC; 2–3 (Alasdair James); 4 (Chris Hepburn); 6t (Chris Hepburn); BC; Liverpool Metropolitan Cathedral: 18bl inset, 19t, 19b; John McIlwain: 9tl, 9br, 10br inset, 12bl, 13bl, 13br, 16–17, 17b, 20bl, 27bl; Mark McNulty: IBC; The Mersey Partnership: 28bl (Wirral MBC), 5tl, 7br, 9cr, 12–13, 13tr (The Beatles Story), 15tr, 25b, 27tl, 27r, 28tr (Peter Owen/Sefton Tourism), 31; National Museums Liverpool: 5tr, 16c; Pitkin Publishing: 22–23 all (Neil Jinkerson); The World of Glass: 29t.

The publishers would like to thank Jackie Crawford of Liverpool Culture Company; Ed Plent and Sam Vaux of Liverpool Museums; the Mersey Partnership; Dave Jones of The Cavern Club; Kevin Stott of Liverpool Cathedral; and the many staff of various locations mentioned in the guide for their assistance in its preparation.

Written by John McIlwain; the author has asserted his moral rights.
Edited by Clare Collinson and Gill Knappett.
Designed by Tim Noel-Johnson.
Picture research by John McIlwain, Clare Collinson and Gill Knappett.

Maps by PCGraphics (UK) Ltd 2014 (www.pcgraphics.uk.com). Mapping contains Ordnance Survey data © Crown copyright and database right 2014.

PITKIN CITY GUIDES

This guide is just one in a series of city titles
Available by mail order. See our website, **www.pavilionbooks.com**, for our full range of titles, or contact us for a copy of our brochure.

Pitkin Publishing, Pavilion Books Company Limited, 43 Great Ormond Street, London WC1N 3HZ
Enquiries and sales: +44 (0)20 7462 1506
Email: sales@pavilionbooks.com

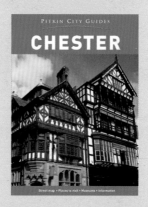

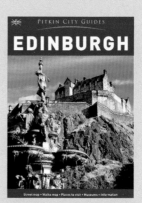

PITKIN

Publication in this form © Pitkin Publishing 2016. An imprint of Pavilion Books Company Limited.

All information correct at time of going to press, but may be subject to change.

Printed in Turkey.
ISBN 978-1-84165-561-1   4/17